DAN SEABORN

D1713150

101 Ways to Love Your Wife

Practical Ways For A Husband to Cherish His Wife.

Encourage Her from A-Z

❧

Beginning with the letter "A" and continuing through the alphabet, list words that characterize your wife. Tell her that she's **A**wesome, **B**eautiful, **C**aring, **D**evoted . . . and so on. If you can't think of a word for some of the harder letters, then make up your own!

Paraphrase Proverbs 31:10-31

Paraphrase Proverbs 31:10-31 and insert your wife's name where appropriate. For example: "I have found a wife of noble character. _____ is worth far more than rubies. _____'s husband has full confidence in her . . ." and so on. Print it and frame it as a special gift to her.

Share Proverbs 19:14 With Your Wife

"Houses and wealth are inherited from parents, but a prudent wife is from the Lord." Tell her the dictionary meaning of the word **prudent** — "wise in handling practical matters" and "careful about one's conduct." Thank her and be grateful for her life of prudence.

4

Rely On Your Strengths

✦

Don't worry if you're not very creative. You'll find some ideas in this book to help you in that area. Concentrate on what you can do instead of what you can't. Help with the cooking, dishes and house cleaning. Get up with the children in the middle of the night when they call. Sit up with your wife when she doesn't feel well. Hold her and let her cry on your shoulder. Find your strength in Christ.

Have a Hidden Language

❧

Create a language that only you and your wife understand. Use hand signals, eye motions or certain words that have meaning for only the two of you. Use your secret language in a crowd to communicate your feelings toward her. She will be delighted that you are thinking of her. For example, three squeezes means "I Love You."

Send a Humorous Card

My friend sent his wife a card that said, "I don't know where to begin to tell you I love you" — open the card — "but I've narrowed it down to either the bedroom or the shower." So buy her a card and send it to her. Don't wait for a special occasion — do it to express your love, to offer encouragement or to make her laugh.

Plan a Surprise Weekend

*A*rrange for all her responsibilities to be taken care of and pack the necessary items for a weekend away. Surprise her by picking her up at work or at home and whisk her away to her favorite place. Make sure that all bases are covered. This weekend should be as worry-free as possible.

Hold Her Hand

*W*hen you're walking together, slip up beside her and take her hand. It makes her feel special and creates unity. Others will see your commitment to each other through this simple act of love.

Use Positive Phrases

B uild self-esteem. Some examples are:

"You've made me the happiest man in the world."
"Our children are blessed to have a mom like you."
"I love you."
"You're beautiful."
"You're a great mother."
"How did your day go?"

Send a Single Red Rose

*B*egin a tradition of sending her a single red rose on some particular day. Send it on the same day every year. Let it become your own holiday. Consider taking this day off work because of its significance.

Take a Walk

*O*n the spur of the moment, ask your wife to join you for a walk. Stroll on the beach, to the end of the pier, down a favorite street, into the park — wherever you know she is peaceful. Talk about life and how much you love her. Sometime during the walk, kiss her softly . . . with no ulterior motive.

Leave a Note

As you leave for work, put a note on the bathroom mirror reminding her of your love and telling her you'll be thinking of her today. Leave notes in other places where you know she will find them.

Rent a Hot Tub

*C*all a rental service or a hot-tub dealer and tell them you want to try one out for the weekend. Get it all set up in your backyard and show your wife the surprise. (You'll probably end up buying the thing, so be prepared.)

Initiate a Love Attack

❧

$\mathcal{E}$ very once in a while, give in to the urge to "attack" your wife in a loving way and wrestle her to the floor. Be playful and fun and don't do anything that makes her feel uncomfortable. Let her pin you down and win the fight. If you have small children, don't frighten them with this type behavior. Be thoughtful — if she's all dressed up and looking beautiful, plan your "love attack" for another time.

Build a Fire

*T*reat your wife to a glass of sparkling grape juice and have her sit in front of the fireplace. Build a fire and use one of those glowsticks that create beautiful colors in the flames. Tell her she's more beautiful than all the colors in the world. Name a quality about her you admire for every color you can see in the fire. Share a bowl of popcorn and enjoy the quiet moment together.

Do An Odd Job

Surprise your wife by doing that one job that has been waiting to be done for a long time — you know which one it is.   Don't delay another minute . . . go to the store, get the supplies and do it.

Date

*A*sk your wife out on a date every two weeks. Let it be a time of fun and relaxation. It doesn't have to be expensive . . . even a simple picnic will be enjoyable and creative. Be sure to make arrangements for child care if necessary.

18

Memorize
Ephesians 5:25

"*H*usbands, love your wives, just as Christ loved the church and gave himself up for her." Put it into practice.

Have a "Top 5" List

Give your wife the opportunity to share five things she wants you to improve about yourself. Ask her to pray for you and dedicate yourself to prayer for growth in these areas.

Go to Bed Early

For communication purposes only, turn off the television and put down the newspaper and go to bed with your wife. Share a time of holding each other and talking about your day before fading into sleep.

Pray For Her

L ist the top five needs, from your perspective, of your wife. Keep the list in a private place and refer to it during your quiet time with God. He can do wonderful things for her through your prayers.

Pray With Her

take time each day to pray together. If you don't work at it, it won't happen. The benefits of effective and fervent prayer with your wife are immeasurable. God will bless your marriage and strengthen it with His love.·

Survive The Drudgery

*L*augh a little as you read Ecclesiastes 9:9. "Enjoy life with your wife, whom you love, all the days of this meaningless life that God has given you under the sun — all your meaningless days . . ." Your wife can encourage and inspire you during those pointless days. Enjoy her humor and wisdom and look forward to the life God has for you.

Try Love Listening

❧

*W*hen your wife is talking to you, look at her and listen carefully. Be thinking about what she is saying and absorb each word rather than preparing your counter statement. When you truly listen, each conversation will deepen your love for each other.

Don't Manipulate

*B*e sensitive to your wife's needs all the time, not just when you want something from her. Mutual honesty and caring along with unselfish actions will bring trust and confidence to the relationship.

Tally Your Victories

*G*ood marriages face tough times. Usually, the problems are of little significance. Rather than focusing on the battles, learn to count the victories. Celebrate each one. Overcoming each conflict will make you stronger for the battles ahead.

Rent a Sign

*R*ent one of those big flashing white signs and put it in the front yard. Put the phrase "America's Greatest Wife" or "Wife of the Year" on it in big black letters. The neighborhood will love it and though your wife may be embarrassed, inside she will know you care.

A Scriptural Blessing

Proverbs 5:18-19: "May your fountain be blessed, and may you rejoice in the wife of your youth. A loving doe, a graceful deer—may her breasts satisfy you always, may you ever be captivated by her love." Let this be your theme verse for the week.

Remind Yourself of 1 Peter 3:7

"Husbands, in the same way be considerate as you live with your wives, and treat them with respect as the weaker partner and as heirs with you of the gracious gift of life, so that nothing will hinder your prayers." Note that last part — the way you love your wife has a direct bearing on the effectiveness of your prayers.

Do The Laundry

*G*ather all the dirty clothes and separate the light colors from the dark colors. Read the instructions on the laundry detergent and wash all the dirty clothes. After drying, fold them and put them away. Not only will you be a great help, but your eyes will be opened to the types of things your wife does that go unnoticed. Thank her and consider helping her from now on with this responsibility.

Practice Sacrifice

*E*phesians 5:28 says, "In this same way, husbands ought to love their wives as their own bodies. He who loves his wife loves himself." Whom do you love the most?

Make a Video

*C*reate a video that encourages her. Interview several people who love her and let them share what she means to them. End the video with your comments, affirming what the others have said and adding your own thoughts. To surprise her, pretend you've rented a video for her to watch. When you pop it in . . . it's especially for her.

Make a "Top 10" List

*M*ake a list of the top ten reasons you remember falling in love with your wife. Share it with her. Evaluate your relationship — are you still falling in love? Why or why not? What can you do to keep the love flowing?

Give Her Freedom

❧

*Y*our wife needs to feel free to make decisions that affect her life. She deals constantly with issues at home, at work and at school that require her to make choices. She will value your opinion more if you don't force it on her. Don't pressure her into an answer. Discuss her options openly, then leave it up to her to resolve the issue.

Don't Make Excuses

*I*f you're justifying your actions, you're losing. Instead of making excuses to cover yourself, own up to the facts of the situation, apologize and get on with life. Your excuses will only bring your wife frustration, but your honesty will cause her to respect you.

Stop Whining When You're Sick

*W*e men are usually worse than children, aren't we? We make loud, moaning noises to get attention. We ask for all sorts of favors and pretend like we're going to die. When women get sick, they just keep working. Learn to take your sickness in stride — without the whining and complaining — and your wife will be forever grateful.

Encourage Openness

※

*C*reate an environment in which your wife feels free to share her true feelings. Honesty and openness — without fear of rebuke — will build your relationship and give her confidence. Women need to share their feelings with those they love. Anytime your wife feels free to be honest, you win!

Build a Reserve

*M*y car has a reserve tank. When the little light on the instrument panel comes on, I know there's enough gas to go fifty miles. Build a reserve tank for your wife for those times when the feelings aren't there or the disagreement is "hot and heavy." Switch to your reserve tank by calling on the Lord and reminding yourself why you said "I DO." Be faithful to your commitment.

Change

As you become aware of areas in your life that need to change in order to improve your relationship . . . act on it. Here are three simple steps:

    a. Admit the need.
    b. Accept responsibility for the change.
    c. Plan your next steps and have another friend hold you accountable.

Let your wife give her input into your actions. Think of an area now and start the process.

Admire Her Positive Attributes

L ist your wife's top five wonderful attributes. Find a way during your normal course of conversation to compliment her on these qualities. Next week, think of five more and continue your praise of her.

Say "I Love You" With Your Actions

*T*ake out the trash. Change a light bulb. Fix a hole in the wall. Put the lid down. Pick up your newspapers. Take care of your dirty clothes. Wipe your feet. Do all of this without being asked.

Share Your Feelings

❧

*T*his a tough one for us men, because we'd rather talk about football and the weather than the way we feel. But your wife is the one who has agreed to spend her life with you. She needs to know of your hopes and dreams, your fears and your feelings of inadequacy. She will become a tremendous source of support if you will share with her what's in your heart.

Say YES

When your wife asks if you're available to help her, say YES. When she needs someone to go with her to the store, say YES. When she needs someone to help with the children, say YES. Saying yes will build positive thoughts about you and about your involvement in her life. It will also deepen her reserve supply of love for you. Life has enough NO's . . . say YES.

Hide Some Chocolate

✦

Stash little pieces of chocolate or her favorite candy in places where you know your wife will find them. Attach a note that reminds her of your love.

Hug More

For no reason, out of the blue, hug your wife. Do it often. A simple hug is a terrific way to relay confidence, affirmation, pride and support. Count it a blessing to have a spouse who is affectionate.

Relieve Her of Worry

❧

*I*f your wife tends to worry, seek to build her trust by reminding her of God's love and provision. Share with her Matthew 6:27, "Who of you by worrying can add a single hour to his life?" Continue to read the next few verses and see how He cares for the flowers and the birds. Take a walk together and enjoy His flowers and His birds.

Leave a Message

✷

*C*all her voice mail service or the answering machine and leave an anonymous love note. Try to disguise your voice. Don't scare her, just think of a unique and creative way to let her know you are thinking about her.

Watch Her Sleep

I usually go to bed after my wife is asleep. Sometimes I look at her as she peacefully sleeps. I pray for her and think about how blessed I am to have her as my wife. Before I turn out the lights I gently kiss her cheek. Do that!

Help Her With Commitments

❦

Wives seem to have many diverse responsibilities. How many men do you know who volunteer at school, bake cookies for the bake sale, help with homework, make a dozen phone calls and balance the checkbook — all in one day? Is there one of those tasks that you could do for her? Why not lighten her load a bit? Look for your opportunity today.

Defend Her

*I*n the presence of others, speak only positively of your wife. Make it a point to say only good things behind her back. Expect the same from others. Uplift her name and reputation. Make sure that belittling isn't allowed in the family. Let her know you hold her in highest esteem.

Special Bouquet Day

*O*n a spring day, collect flowers on the way home and present them to her as a special present. Take time to name each flower and tell her where you found it and why it reminds you of her.

Tell Her You Like Her

❧

*Y*ou and your wife have some obvious differences. There may be times when she's not sure you like her much, even though she knows you love her. Take a moment to tell her all the things you like about her. She needs to hear that every so often.

Say "Thank You"

*I*n most homes the wife cooks, cleans, guides, mothers, loves, comforts, encourages, chauffeurs . . . and the list goes on. Wow! What a lady! Have you ever thought about how you would make it without her? Tell her of your gratitude.

Go to a Play

❧

*L*et her pick her favorite play and take her to the production even if you think you won't enjoy it. Who knows — you might find yourself getting wrapped up in the plot and the music. Afterward, share the exciting moments of the play over a hot fudge sundae. You will go home refreshed and exhilarated.

Pothole
Car Washes

ome wives have the unique ability to hit every pothole in the road. If you can imagine these potholes as miniature car washes and she's trying to help keep the car clean, it's easy to deal with. Every little splash is her way of saying she loves helping you. Have this attitude and enjoy the potholes.

Get One-On-One

With today's busy lifestyles, it is difficult for husbands and wives to find time to get together one-on-one. But focusing on each other and sharing intimate conversation is necessary for healthy growth in marriage. Find time today to be alone with your wife. Share events of the day, talk about your feelings, make plans for the future. Nothing beats being alone with the one you love.

Give Car Crash Gifts

*E*ach time your wife dents a fender or backs into a tree, send her a bouquet of flowers to remind her that she is more important than the car. Remember Matthew 6:19 which says, "Do not store up for yourselves treasures on earth . . ." Instead, store your value in her . . . the treasure of a lifetime.

Enjoy Her Cooking

I marvel at my wife's ability to think through a week's worth of meals for our entire family. I enjoy almost every meal she prepares. If the roles were reversed, I know we would have to eat out a lot to keep all the troops satisfied. Thank your wife and enjoy the meals she prepares.

59

Honor Her Goals

*D*o you know your wife's goals and aspirations? If not, take time to
find out what they are. Discuss them with her and encourage her
to accomplish each one. Assist in whatever way you can.

If She's Pregnant

*W*hen or if she's pregnant, tell her she is beautiful. Women often struggle with the "big" look. Help convince her God gave her that butterball look and therefore it's gorgeous. Just for fun . . . dress up like a pregnant lady and go out to dinner together. Laugh . . . lots of other people will.

Hire a Cleaning Lady

*M*ost women don't enjoy housecleaning, even though they do it all the time. Try hiring a cleaning lady for a week or two. Ask her to do some of the tougher jobs, such as waxing the floor and washing windows. Let her work while you take your wife out to a movie or an ice cream cone. Even if you can't afford to do this often, your thoughtfulness will not go unnoticed.

Give a Good-Bye Hug and Kiss

❧

*T*his old favorite is hard to beat. There are no guarantees that you will get another chance to show your love. Always leave your wife with a hug and a kiss, so that her last memory of you will be one of love.

Massage Her Feet

❧

After you've had a long day, seek to test your servanthood by slowly massaging her feet. Let her relax in her favorite chair with a book or just let her close her eyes. When she's completely satisfied . . . massage for five more minutes. Then thank her for letting you do it.

Compliment Her Home

*N*otice the times she cleans the house or rearranges the furniture. Walk through the room and appreciate her decorating skills. After showering her with compliments . . . if no kids are around . . . invite her to the couch and do what comes naturally.

Admire Her Haircut

❧

*W*hen your wife returns from a hair appointment, check out her new "do." Compliment her on it and let her know she's beautiful. If you're one of those men who never notices, wake up and take notice!

Try Something New

To keep the spark alive — to keep her guessing what's next — take her somewhere she's never been or do something she's never done before. Go horseback riding, try out the zoo, hike through the mountains — whatever you do, enjoy the thrill of new experiences together.

Build Her Confidence

*E*very woman is gifted in some way — most of them have many talents. Look for opportunities to tell your wife how gifted she is. Focus on those little talents that make her so special. Find a way to work your compliments into the conversation.

Don't Sweat The Mess

❧

Some wives get craftsy around Christmas time or other special holidays and let their crafts scatter all through the house. Don't fuss about it. Instead, help her make something. Do the detail work. Stop worrying about the mess and enjoy her hobby with her.

Laugh More

L aughter can cure a world of hurts. Take advantage of every opportunity to bring laughter into the home. Life is too short for us to be serious all the time. Tell jokes, play pranks, enjoy the silly nonsense of your children or create some silly nonsense of your own. You will be amazed at how laughter eases the tension and makes the home a better place for everyone.

Show Respect

he dictionary says that to respect someone is to consider them worthy of high regard. You wife is worthy of your esteem and honor. Respect her in every way — her views, her ideas, her individuality and her abilities deserve your highest regard. Respect her!

Handle Discipline

Your wife needs an abundance of encouragement and support in dealing with the children. Seek to deal with discipline problems when they arise and avoid placing this responsibility solely on her. Children need to see their parents united in their efforts to uphold the rules of the family. Be firm, but gentle. Make sure your rules are based on God's laws, not on your own wants and needs.

Buy a Novel

❧

*I*f your wife likes to read, purchase the latest book by her favorite author. Present her with this gift at dinner time. Then offer to do the dishes while she curls up in a chair to enjoy her present. You'll show her that you recognize her need for relaxation and prove to her that she is high on your list of priorities.

Prepare a Bubble Bath

✿

After dinner, excuse yourself and prepare a warm bath with perfumed bubbles. Lay out a towel with mints and escort her to this unexpected surprise. If she desires, help her undress. Assure her that you will take care of her other responsibilities so she can relax for a while.

Help The Kids With Homework

❧

Somehow, the burden of assisting the children with their homework usually falls to mothers. Plan on helping your wife with this responsibility during the school week. Nothing quite matches the joy of working together to teach your children. Who knows, you might even learn something!

Leave Lipstick On The Mirror

*L*eave a message in lipstick for your wife on the bathroom mirror. Something like . . . "My lips can't wait to meet yours" or "Kiss me and you've kissed the best." Life is short — play a little.

Remember The First Time

⸎

R eminisce together about your first date or the first time you met. Recall some of the silly things you did. Be prepared for both laughter and tears as old memories are brought to light. Remind her that you are as much in love with her today as you were back then.

Take Her Shopping

$\mathcal{S}$et aside a Saturday morning and devote it to driving her to her favorite stores. Patiently wait while she tries on different outfits and give her your opinion on each one. Let her decide which one she likes best, then surprise her by purchasing it for her.

Visit a Grave

*t might sound a bit unusual, but consider taking your wife to the gravesite of someone who had great influence on her life. Have her recall the memories and the heritage that was passed on to her. Share with her how you see those beautiful characteristics in her life. Remind each other of the example you're setting for your children and others around you.

Admit Your Mistakes

❧

$\mathcal{D}$on't get into the rut of blaming others and never taking responsibility for your mistakes. The Bible teaches us that the husband is to love his wife as Christ loved the church. As you admit your mistakes, you implement Christ's example of humility and servanthood into your home and your relationship.

Go One Week

*W*ithout telling your wife, plan on a week of only encouraging and supportive comments, never allowing yourself to get frustrated or share hurtful statements. By the fifth day, your wife will wonder what's going on. It should not surprise her when days pass without criticism. It should be commonplace. Continue to practice this until it becomes the standard in your home.

Don't Argue

*T*hough it's easier said than done, if you can agree to disagree on certain issues, you both win. Once you start slipping down the slide of argument, the battle only intensifies and the result is a messy pile-up at the bottom. Deciding not to argue takes discipline and determination. Give it your best shot.

Get Organized

Never be caught off guard because of your failure to communicate with your wife. Put your appointments on her calendar. Know when doctor and dentist visits are scheduled. Become familiar with the household routines. Make a "to do" list of jobs that need to be done around the house, and begin working on them one at a time. Give your home life higher priority than your working life.

Memorize
Proverbs 16:9

❧

"*I*n his heart a man plans his course, but the Lord determines his steps." He will guide your relationship with your spouse as you trust every step to Him.

Send Secret Signals

*E*stablish a secret signal — a nod of the head, a wink of the eye, or some such motion — that means something special to the two of you. Using your secret signals allows you to share an intimate moment no matter where you are.

Reminisce

❧

Spend time talking about your past. Recall memories of your
childhood, the birth of your children, silly incidents along the way.
Think about God's provision for your lives. Discuss what memories you
are leaving for your children. It's important not to lose sight of those
incidents that shaped your life and made you who you are today.

Be On Time

If you and your wife have a prearranged appointment, make sure you are at the specified place on time. Even if others have to wait, or if you have to leave a meeting early . . . be there for her. She deserves the firstfruits of your time. Others will go in and out of your life . . . she is yours to cherish forever.

Rent Costumes

❧

*F*or a fun evening, borrow or rent costumes and go out on the town. Batman and Robin . . . Fred and Wilma . . . Oscar and Mayer . . . whatever. Go to your friends' houses and deliver little gag gifts. Just enjoy life together. Eat at McDonald's, or if your face is disguised, the elite restaurant in town . . . or out of town.

Give a Back Rub

❧

*I*nvite your wife to sit down in front of you and give her tired shoulders a slow, soothing massage. Then fix her a warm cup of coffee or cocoa and ask her about her day.

Give Her What She Needs

❧

Seek to fulfill your wife's needs when it comes to physical intimacy. Ask her what she wants. Find out what makes her feel good. Pay more attention to her desires than you do to your own. Surprisingly enough, you will be more than satisfied as you endeavor to satisfy her.

90

keep a Journal

*W*rite down what you do as a couple every day. Include both good times and bad. From time to time, look back and recall some great moments and share how other not-so-great moments have strengthened your relationship.

Write a Poem

*E*xpress your feelings about your wife in poetry. Use rhyming words, comparisons and metered phrases. If you can, put your words to music. At a special time, read your poem — or sing your song — for her ears only.

A Pig's What?

Proverbs 11:22 says, "Like a gold ring in a pig's snout is a beautiful woman who shows no discretion." Thank your wife for her discretion and remind her of a time you've seen her use it. Ask her if you can place her wedding ring on her finger again. Thank her for wearing her ring on her hand instead of her nose.

Make Birthdays Special

Don't just give your wife a card or a new set of dishes on her birthday. Do something that makes the whole day special for her. Take her out to her favorite restaurant . . . invite her friends over for cake and ice cream . . . send her flowers . . . buy her a new dress. As you go to bed that night, pull one last surprise gift from under her pillow and enjoy watching her open it. Go to sleep hugging. Be as creative as you can — just don't let the day go by unnoticed.

Have Fun With Scripture

*A*sk your wife to adopt Song of Songs 5:3 as her theme verse. It states: "I have taken off my robe — must I put it on again?" Read on in this passage . . . it only gets better. Be thankful God understood our desire for our wives and gave us His word to prove it.

Guard Yourself

*T*ake care to be on your guard against sexual temptation. Proverbs 6:23-35 compares adultery to walking on hot coals or scooping them up. Neither can be done without suffering great pain. If you find yourself tempted to have an adulterous relationship, be warned of the harm it will do you and your family. You might as well set yourself on fire. According to the Bible, it's almost the same thing.

Set Long-Term Goals

$\mathcal{T}$ ake time to establish some marriage goals. Find out what your wife wants to accomplish in the marriage relationship. Blend your ideas into some definable goals. Post them on the refrigerator and evaluate your progress regularly.

Send Her Home

*P*lan a time for her to spend with her family. Work with your in-laws to make it a special surprise. Be sure to make arrangements for her daily responsibilities so she can relax and enjoy her trip.

Carve a tree

❦

Remember when you were a teenager and you carved your girlfriend's initials along with your own into the bark of a tree? Do it again, only this time use your wife's initials. Show her your masterpiece. Tie a ribbon around the tree to mark its significance. You'll be surprised how many people will ask you about it, giving you the opportunity to tell them how much you love your wife. And hey . . . be careful with that knife.

Give Her a Sense of Belonging

*Y*our wife needs to feel that she is an important and necessary part of the home — not just because of the work she does, but because of who she is — your wife. If you do not provide this, she may begin to look elsewhere for fulfillment. Spend more time at mealtimes talking about the day's experiences. Relax and refresh each other with conversation. Make bedtime peaceful and delightful. Give her the gift of your time and she will be loyal and contented.

Do Something Nice

*A*sk your wife to join you in doing something nice for someone else without getting caught. Build your sense of teamwork by participating together in this act of servanthood. Keep the secret just between yourselves.

Begin Again

*S*tart over . . . listen again . . . pray again . . . fold clothes again . . . surprise her again . . . journal again . . . again and again. Never quit loving your wife. She is a gift from God, a treasure to be cherished for all time.

What Are My Five Favorite Memories With My Wife?

1.

2.

3.

4.

5.